PIANO / VOCAL / GUITAR

Robert Johnson
COMPLETE

Cover Photography ©1989 Delta Haze Corporation
Used by Permission

ISBN 0-634-05656-5

HAL•LEONARD®
CORPORATION
7777 W. BLUEMOUND RD. P.O. BOX 13819 MILWAUKEE, WI 53213

Visit Hal Leonard Online at
www.halleonard.com

COME ON IN MY KITCHEN

Words and Music by
ROBERT JOHNSON

DEAD SHRIMP BLUES

Words and Music by
ROBERT JOHNSON

gog-gle-eyed perch-es _____ and they bar-be-cu-in' the bone. _____

Now you've tak-en my shrimp, ba-by, _____ you know you turned me down.

I could-n't do noth-in' un-til I got my-self un-wound. You've

CROSS ROAD BLUES
(Crossroads)

Words and Music by
ROBERT JOHNSON

Moderate Rocking Blues

I went to the

cross - road, ___ fell down on my ___ knees. ___

went to the cross - road, ___ fell down on my ___ knees. ___

Asked the Lord a-bove "Have mer - cy, _____

save __ poor __ Bob, if you please." _____

Mmm, stand - in' at the cross - road, _

I tried to flag a ride. _____

Stand-in' at the cross -

- road,___ I ___ tried to flag a ___ ride.___

Ain't no - bod - y seem to know me,___

DRUNKEN HEARTED MAN

Words and Music by
ROBERT JOHNSON

FROM FOUR UNTIL LATE

Words and Music by
ROBERT JOHNSON

From four ___ un-til late ___ I was wring-in' my hands ___ and cryin'.

From four ___ un-til late ___ I was wring-

in' my hands ___ and cryin'. ___

I be-lieve ___

31

HELL HOUND ON MY TRAIL

Words and Music by
ROBERT JOHNSON

All I need's my li'l sweet wom- an

and to keep my com- pa- ny, _____ hmm, _____ hmm, hmm, hmm, _____

my com- pa- ny. _____

HONEYMOON BLUES

Words and Music by
ROBERT JOHNSON

I BELIEVE I'LL DUST MY BROOM

Words and Music by
ROBERT JOHNSON

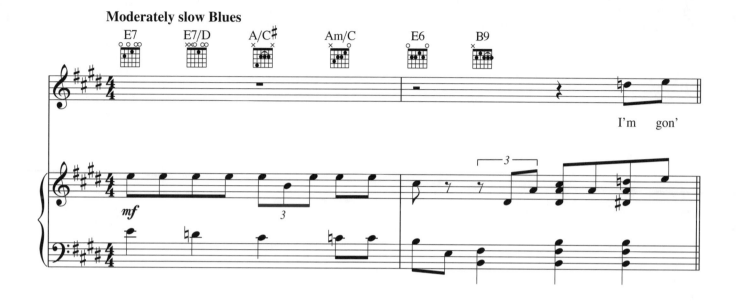

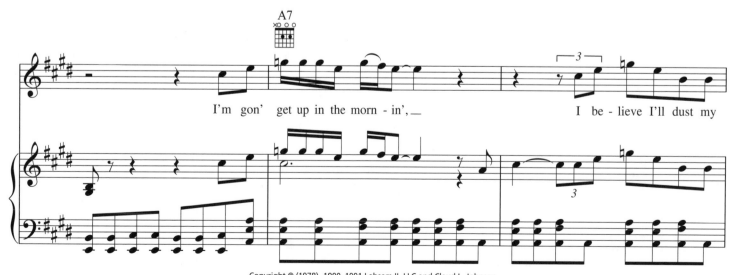

KIND HEARTED WOMAN BLUES

Words and Music by
ROBERT JOHNSON

I'M A STEADY ROLLIN' MAN
(Steady Rollin' Man)

Words and Music by
ROBERT JOHNSON

Moderate Blues

I'm a stead-y roll-in' man,

I roll ___ both night and day. ___

I'm a stead-y roll-in' man, ___ hmm, ___

have been for man-y long years I know.

And some cream puff's us-in' my mon-ey, ooh well babe,

but that'll nev-er be no more.

You can't give your sweet wom-an

ev - 'ry - thing she wants in one time._____

D/A

Ohh - hoo,_ you can't give your sweet wom - an _____

A7   A7sus

ev - 'ry - thing she wants in one time._____

A7   E/B

Well boys, she get ram - blin' in her brain,_ hmm,_ hmm,

some oth - er man on _____ her mind. _____

I'm a stead - y roll - in' man, _____

I roll _____ both night _____ and day. _____

I am a stead - y roll - in' man,

IF I HAD POSSESSION OVER JUDGMENT DAY

Words and Music by
ROBERT JOHNSON

And I went to the __ moun - tain look - in'

far as my eyes __ could see, __

and I __ went to the moun -

my arms____ and I____ slow - ly walked__ a - way.____

Spoken: I didn't like the way she done.

I had to fold____ my arms_

____ and I slow - ly walked a - way.____

Now run here, ba - by,_____ set down_____ on my knee._____

Now run here, ba - by, set down on_____ my knee._____

LAST FAIR DEAL GONE DOWN

Words and Music by
ROBERT JOHNSON

84

That ding - dong keeps ring - in' so soon.

And that ding - dong keeps ring - in' so

soon, good Lord, on that Gulf - and - Port Is - land Road.

LOVE IN VAIN BLUES

Words and Music by
ROBERT JOHNSON

LITTLE QUEEN OF SPADES

Words and Music by
ROBERT JOHNSON

Moderately slow Blues

Now, she is the lit-tle queen of spades ___

and the men will not ___ let her be. ___

Hmm, hmm, ___ she's the lit-tle queen of spades

MALTED MILK

Words and Music by
ROBERT JOHNSON

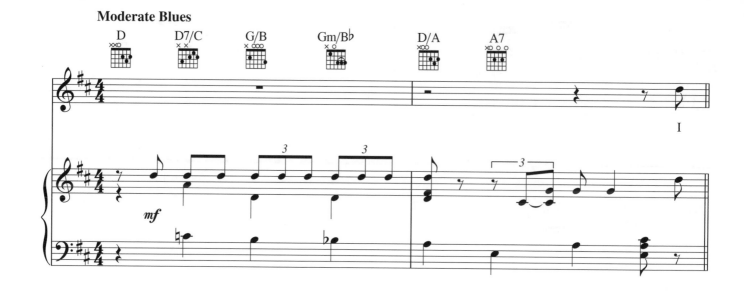

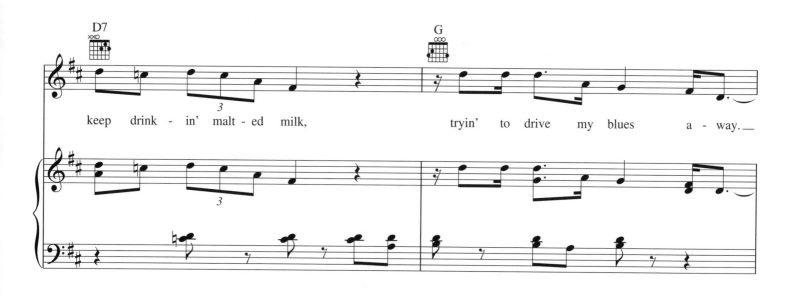

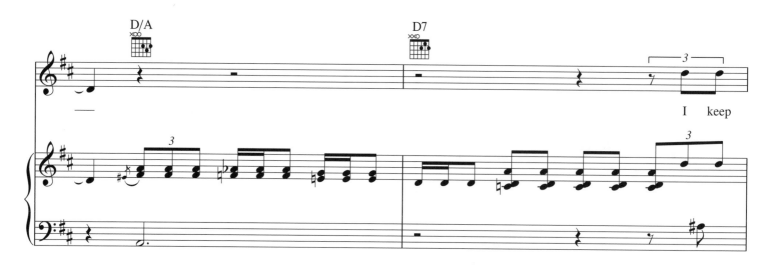

ME AND THE DEVIL BLUES

Words and Music by
ROBERT JOHNSON

MILKCOW'S CALF BLUES

Words and Music by
ROBERT JOHNSON

SWEET HOME CHICAGO

Words and Music by
ROBERT JOHNSON

Original key: F# major. This edition has been transposed up one half-step to be more playable.

PHONOGRAPH BLUES

Words and Music by
ROBERT JOHNSON

Original key: B major. This edition has been transposed up one half-step to be more playable.

bring your clothes back home, and try me one more time.

She got a pho-no-graph, and it won't say a lone-some word.

She

PREACHIN' BLUES
(Up Jumped the Devil)

Words and Music by
ROBERT JOHNSON

heard __

blues   walk - in'   like   a   man. __

I's   up   this   morn', __

heard blues walk-in' like a man.____

Wor - ried blues,____

give me____ your right hand.____

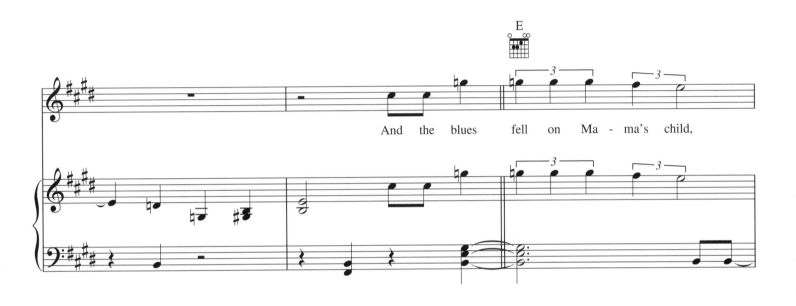

And the blues fell on Ma - ma's child,

tore up all up - side down.

Blues __

__ fell on Ma-ma's child, ____ and it

tore me all ____ up - side down.

Trav-el on, poor Bob, ____

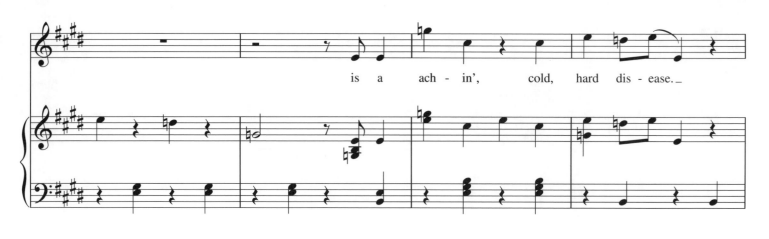

is a ach - in', cold, hard dis - ease.

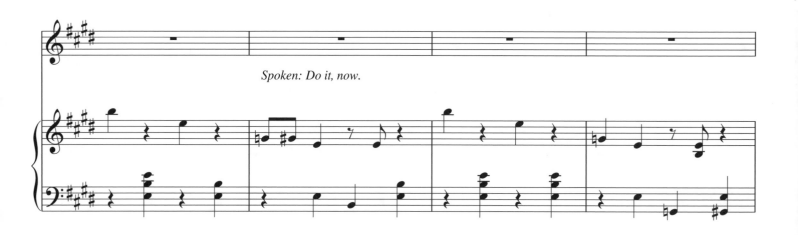

Spoken: Do it, now.

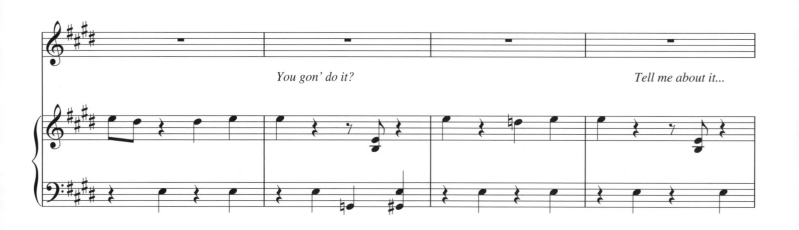

You gon' do it?

Tell me about it...

stud - yin' and read - in'. ___   I'm 'on'

drive ___ my blues a - way.

Go - in' to the 'stil' - ry, ___

(Half-tempo)

E7/B   A/C#   Am/C   E/B   E

stay out ___ there all day.

RAMBLIN' ON MY MIND

Words and Music by
ROBERT JOHNSON

Original key: F♯ major. This edition has been transposed up one half-step to be more playable.

STONES IN MY PASSWAY

Words and Music by
ROBERT JOHNSON

Moderately slow Blues

I got stones in my pass-way,

and my road___ seem dark at night.___

I got stones in my pass-way,

and my road seem dark at night.

N.C.

I have pains in my heart,_____

A7

they have tak - en my ap - pe - tite.__

I have a bird to whis - tle

and all my lov-in', too.___ You laid a pass-way fun-ny.___ Now,

what are you try-ing to do?___ I'm cry-in' please,___

please___ let us be friends.___

And when you hear me howl-in' in my pass-way, rid-er,

please___ o - pen your door and let me in. _____

I got three legs to truck home,

boys, __ please don't block my road. _____

A7

D7

I got three legs __ to truck home, _____

STOP BREAKIN' DOWN BLUES

Words and Music by
ROBERT JOHNSON

THEY'RE RED HOT

Words and Music by
ROBERT JOHNSON

Hot ta - ma - les and they're red hot, yes, she got 'em for sale. ___

Hot ta - ma - les and they're red hot, yes, she got 'em for sale. ___

I got a girl, said she long and tall, ___ she sleeps in the kitch-en with her

Original Key: Db major. This edition has been transposed down one half-step to be more playable.

32-20 BLUES

Words and Music by
ROBERT JOHNSON

'F I send ___ for my ba - by, and she don't ___ come, ___ 'f I send ___ for my ba - by, man, and she don't come,

you ain't talk - in' ___ right. ___ Got a thir -

ty - eight spe - cial, boys, it do ver - y well. ___

Got a thir - ty - eight spe - cial, boys, it do ver - y well. ___

___ I got a thir - ty - two - twen - ty, now, and

TRAVELING RIVERSIDE BLUES

Words and Music by
ROBERT JOHNSON

to Rose - dale, gon - na take my rid - er by my side. _____

Well, I'm go - in'

We can still _____ bar - rel house, _____ ba - by, 'cause it's on the

WALKIN' BLUES

Words and Music by
ROBERT JOHNSON

Original key: B major. This edition has been transposed up one half-step to be more playable.

some peo-ple tell me that the wor-ried blues ain't bad. ____ Worst ____ old ____ feel-in' I most ____

ev-er ____ had. ____ Some peo-ple tell me that these ____ old wor-ried old blues ain't bad. __

____ It's the ____ worst old ____ feel-in' ____

I ____ most ev-er had. She got a

WHEN YOU GOT A GOOD FRIEND

Words and Music by
ROBERT JOHNSON

Original key: F♯ major. This edition has been transposed up one half-step to be more playable.

Watch your close__ friends ba - by, __ then your en - e - mies can't__ do you no harm. __

When you got a good friend _____ that will stay right by__ your_ side, _____

TERRAPLANE BLUES

Words and Music by
ROBERT JOHNSON

Original key: B major. This edition has been transposed up one half-step to be more playable.

your horn won't e - ven blow.

Spoken: Somebody's been runnin' my

batteries down on this machine.

I e - ven flashed my lights, ma - ma

this horn won't e - ven blow.____

Got a short in this con - nec - tion,

I'm 'bout to check your oil.

C7

N.C.

I got a wom-an that I'm lov-in'

C7

way down in Ar-kan-sas.

Now, you know the coils ain't e-ven buzz-in',___ lit-tle

driv - in' my Ter - ra-plane, now, for you_____ since I been gone?_____

I'm gon' get deep

down in this con - nec - tion,_____ keep on tan - glin' with your wires.

I'm gon'